War in the Gulf

AFTER THE STORM

Written By: Bob Italia

Published by Abdo & Daughters, 6535 Cecelia Circle, Edina, Minnesota 55439.

Library bound edition distributed by Rockbottom Books,
Pentagon Tower, P.O. Box 36036, Minneapolis, Minnesota 55435.

Printed in the United States.

Cover photo: Bettman Archive
Inside photos: Bettman Archive 4, 7, 14, 17, 23, 25, 32, 41, 43

Edited by: Rosemary Wallner

Italia, Robert, 1955-
    After the storm / written by Bob Italia.
    p. cm. -- (War in the Gulf)
    Summary: Discusses the Persian Gulf War, including the air war, the ground war,
and the aftermath.
ISBN: 1-56239-147-X (lib bdg)
1. Persian Gulf War, 1991—Juvenile literature. [1. Persian Gulf War, 1991.] I.
Wallner, Rosemary, 1964-   . II. Title. III. Series.
DS79.723.I82 1992   956.704'.42--dc20   92-17392

International Standard	**Library of Congress**
Book Number:	**Catalog Card Number:**
1-56239-147-X	92-17392

TABLE OF CONTENTS

With the help of Apache attack helicopters,
Operation Desert Storm ended swiftly.

A CLOSER LOOK AT
OPERATION DESERT STORM

Operation Desert Storm was a huge success. It began January 16, 1991. It ended February 27, 1991. In that short time, Allied forces drove the Iraqi army from Kuwait, a small country on the Persian Gulf.

The final blow came from the 100-hour ground war. U.S. General Norman Schwarzkopf led the ground war. The ground troops surrounded the Iraqis. Then they attacked them with a fast moving armored assault.

The entire world watched the war live on television. There were many exciting moments. The "smart" bombs. The Scuds. But television told only part of the story. Operation Desert Storm wasn't as easy to complete as it seemed. Many secrets and facts did not appear until after the war.

Despite the war's success, not much has changed in the Persian Gulf. Iraq and Kuwait are slowly rebuilding. They hope to regain their prewar life. Saddam Hussein remains in power in Iraq. He is still a threat to Middle East countries.

THE AIR WAR

The TV images of the air war were vivid. There didn't seem to be much of an air war at all. It was so one-sided. The Iraqi Air Force was nowhere in sight. Many of its pilots were too afraid to fight the Allied Air Force. When they did, they were shot down instantly. The hapless Iraqi air defense guns fired aimlessly into the night sky over Baghdad, Iraq.

Meanwhile, Allied bombers and fighters flew unharmed to their targets. Smart bombs found their way into doors and air shafts before exploding. The bombers and fighters returned to base without a scratch. They were ready to reload and fly another mission.

Because the skies over Baghdad were heavily defended,
only the F-117 Stealth fighters bombed the city.

But the air war was not so easy. In the war's early
stages, Allied pilots often engaged the Iraqi Air Force
in tense and deadly dogfights. The Allies also feared
the heavily-defended skies over Baghdad. That's why
only the F-117 Stealth fighters—invisible to radar—
bombed the city. The large number of Allied aircraft
used—the greatest in military history—finally defeated
the Iraqi Air Force.

Into the "Hornet's Nest"

In the early morning hours of January 16, 1991, 10 stealth fighters swooped down on Baghdad. They were the first wave of Allied aircraft to strike the city in Operation Desert Storm. The attack caught the Iraqi air defense by surprise.

The Stealth fighters caused great damage to Baghdad. They knocked out electronic communications. They hit Hussein's Presidential Palace. They bombed the Ministry of Defense building. They destroyed the Iraqi Air Force's headquarters.

One smart bomb hit the *top* of a 320-foot tower. The bomb destroyed all the antennae atop the tower. It did not touch the buildings below.

Two hours later, a wave of 20 Stealth fighters approached Baghdad. This time, the Iraqi air defense was ready. But the gunners could not see the Stealth fighters. So they filled the sky with bursts of bright orange, yellow, and white flak (anti-aircraft fire). Some flak reached a height of 20,000 feet.

"They had stirred up a hornet's nest," said a Stealth pilot. The second wave of fighters would have a tough time getting back safely.

The bursting flak made it hard for the fighters to reach their targets. Because there was so much flak, there was a good chance of getting hit. The pilots ignored the danger around them. They locked onto their targets. They released their bombs. But the bursting flak made it hard to see if the bombs hit their targets. The fighters returned to base safely. Because of the deadly flak, many pilots were surprised that no Stealth fighters had been lost.

Throughout the war, the Stealth fighters flew only 1,271 of the 110,00 combat missions. But their success was amazing. F-117s destroyed almost half of all military targets in Iraq. The Stealth fighters became the heroes of the air war.

To Shoot or Not to Shoot?

The Allies worried about the Iraqi Air Force. The Iraqis had over 500 combat aircraft. Many were made in Russian and France. If the Iraqis wanted to, they could challenge the Allies in the air.

Hours after the first Stealth wave hit Baghdad, F-15 fighters patrolled Iraqi air space. U.S. Air Force Pilot Jon Kelk picked up an electronic blip on his radar. But Kelk wasn't sure if the blip was an Iraqi aircraft or an Allied aircraft. The unknown aircraft was 40 miles away. But Kelk had long-range missiles. Should he shoot or not?

Kelk didn't want to shoot down an Allied aircraft. But what if the aircraft were hostile? If he waited too long to fire, the enemy pilot might shoot first.

Kelk watched the blip closely. It started out low. Then the blip climbed toward him. It looked like the unknown aircraft was about to attack. Kelk got nervous. He called to the nearest AWACS radar controller for help. (AWACS stands for Airborn Warning and Control System.) The controller could not tell whether the unknown aircraft was friend or foe.

Kelk didn't have time to wait. He fired a radar-guided missile. Then he tried to drop his external fuel tanks for a quick escape. The fuel tanks wouldn't release.

A few seconds later, Kelk saw a strange blue flash. He didn't know if he had hit the unknown aircraft, or if the aircraft had fired a missile at him. He veered away from the blue flash. Then he looked at his control panel. The panel showed that none of the F-15's missiles had been fired. Kelk's mind whirled with confusion. Did he fire a missile? If so, did the missile hit its target? And was the target friend or foe?

A day later, Kelk had all his answers. He *had* fired a missile. The unknown aircraft had been an attacking Iraqi MiG. Jon Kelk had scored the first airkill of Operation Desert Storm. He was proud, but he wished it had been much easier.

Other Air War Facts

• "Smart" bombs made up 7 percent of all bombs dropped. The rest were the same type of unguided bomb the military used in Vietnam, Korea, and in World War II.

• The Air Force had few A-10 Warthogs in their air strike fleet. These armor-plated aircraft are slow. Yet the A-10 caused most of the tank kills from the air. Iraqi POWs (Prisoners Of War) said they feared the A-10 the most. It cost $1,106 per hour to fly.

• The Air Force never used its $28 billion fleet of B-1B bombers. The fleet had too many problems. Instead, the 36-year-old B-52 bombers dropped almost 37,000 tons of bombs. The B-52s flew 1,624 missions. None were shot down.

• The Allies fired more than 300 Tomahawk cruise missiles. One Tomahawk costs $1 million.

The Ground War

As with the air war, the ground war quickly uncovered the Iraqis. The news showed starving Iraqi soldiers crawling from foxholes. They begged for food and refused to fight. The Allies took hundreds of prisoners. Allied tank columns smashed through Iraqi defenses. Terrified troops ran for their lives.

Some Iraqi troops—especially the Republican Guard—fought well and hard. Allied soldiers who battled them fought for their lives. Even more, a great tank battle occurred hours before Operation Desert Storm ended.

Though thousands of Iraqi soldiers surrendered,
many did not give up without a fight.

Facing the Tawakalna

Three days after the ground war started, Alpha Troop
headed toward Kuwait's northwest border. Alpha
Troop was ahead of the main invasion force. They had
18 Bradley Fighting Vehicles and no tanks. They
scouted enemy positions. As dusk fell, a sandstorm
blew up. Alpha Troop could see only 300 yards ahead.

Suddenly, Iraqi armored vehicles appeared. Alpha Troop had stumbled upon the Tawakalna (Ta-wa-KALL-na) Division of Iraq's Republican Guard.

The Bradleys opened fire. Captain Gerald Davie, Alpha's commander, saw the shells hit Iraqi armored vehicles. More armored vehicles lay ahead. Because of the blinding sandstorm, Davie could not tell that these armored vehicles were Russian-built T-72 tanks. The Bradleys were no match for the T-72s.

Alpha Troop exchanged rapid fire with the Iraqis. The Iraqi firing was more powerful. "We had no idea how badly we were into it," said Davie. "At that point, we were really just fighting for our lives."

Round after round whizzed past Alpha Troop. Suddenly, a Bradley took a direct hit from a T-72. Ground soldiers pulled the crew from the burning vehicle. The shell mortally wounded the Bradley's gunner, Sergeant Kenneth Gentry. He died fifteen minutes later.

Before Captain Davie could issue a retreat order, Iraqi fire hit another Bradley. Davie called in Alpha Troop's reserves. The reserves covered Alpha Troop while it retreated. But then another Bradley took a direct hit from a T-72, killing its gunner.

Once out of enemy fire, Davie totalled his losses. Enemy fire had killed two men and injured twelve others. Davie also lost five Bradley fighting vehicles. In return, Alpha Troop had destroyed only two Iraqi T-72s. Davie and his men were lucky to be alive.

A Desert Showdown

On February 27, 1991, the U.S. 1st Armored Division's 2nd Brigade rumbled toward the Iraqi army outside Basra, Iraq. The 2nd Brigade was known as the "Iron Brigade." It had 3,000 vehicles. The total included 166 M1A1 Abrams tanks. The M1A1 is the best in the world.

*A great tank battle occurred hours before
Operation Desert Storm ended.*

Just after noon, an Iron Brigade tank gunner spotted
four Iraqi armored vehicles. They were over 2 miles
away. Unknown to the Iron Brigade, they had found
the Republican Guard's Medina Luminous Division.
Medina Luminous was heavily armored. Its main
weapon was the T-72 tank. The T-72 was considered
the M1A1's equal.

From over 2 miles, the Iron Brigade tank gunner fired at the Iraqis. He destroyed two vehicles. Another M1A1 destroyed the other two armored vehicles. The shots were important. Now the Iron Brigade knew they could destroy the enemy from a great distance. The Iraqi T-72s could not return the fire from such a range.

The Iron Brigade drew closer. They could see the Iraqi tanks dug into the desert. The brigade's tank commanders received the order to fire. The M1A1s pounded the Iraqi tanks. By 12:30 p.m., the Iron Brigade had destroyed nearly 30 tanks. The M1A1s hit their targets with amazing accuracy. The T-72s could not.

By 12:50 p.m., the Iron Brigade destroyed 40 Iraqi tanks. By 1 p.m., the battle was over. A few hours later, a cease-fire order officially ended Operation Desert Storm.

"The Battle of Medina Ridge," as it was called, pitted two of the most powerful tanks on Earth. Thanks to its superior firing range, the M1A1 came away with the victory. It truly was the best tank in the world.

"Friendly Fire"

There is often much confusion and tension on the battle-
field. Modern armies can move at great speeds day
and night. Warfare is swift. Aircraft and tanks can
shoot farther than they can see. Sometimes, they don't
know what they are shooting at.

One day before Operation Desert Storm ended,
the U.S. Army attacked the Jalibah Air Base in southern
Iraq. During the attack, an Abrams tank mistook a Bradley for an Iraqi armored vehicle. The Abrams fired a
deadly 120-milimeter shell. The shell killed or wounded
11 U.S. soldiers.

When troops are killed by their own fire, it is officially
called *fratricide* (FRA-tri-cide). Unofficially, the military
calls fratricide "friendly fire." Soldiers don't agree.
"Friendly fire isn't friendly," said a Green Beret Captain.

The Final Toll

When Operation Desert Storm ended, the Defense Intelligence Agency reported 100,000 Iraqi casualties. Since then, the number has been reduced. One report claims that fewer than 8,000 Iraqi soldiers died in Kuwait. Another report places the total Iraqi deaths at 30,000.

American casualties were far less. The Iraqis killed only 148 Americans. Of this total, "friendly fire" killed 35. Unexploded allied bombs killed eleven others. Another 18 American soldiers died from unexploded Iraqi bombs. The unexploded bombs proved deadlier than the Iraqi military.

Other Ground War Facts

• Operation Desert Storm used 2,000 M1A1 Abrams tanks. Enemy fire damaged only eight of them. One high-explosive shell fired by an M1A1 cost between $565 and $1,813.

• Over 16,500 troops, 350 tanks, 200 Bradleys, 200 armored personnel carriers, and 300 other vehicles make up one U.S. armored division. Each division burned 250,000 gallons of fuel per day. Eight divisions burned 8 million gallons of fuel during the 100-hour ground war.

• General Schwarzkopf's monthly pay was $8,485.80. A sergeant's monthly pay is $1,644. A private gets $669 per month.

• Operation Desert Shield cost $76.8 million per day and a total of $12.9 billion.

AFTER THE STORM

A Hero's Welcome

In the 1970s when troops came home after the United States lost the Vietnam War, there were no parades. There were no celebrations. Many war veterans became angry over their treatment. Americans tried to forget the war. Some didn't feel proud of their country.

Operation Desert Storm changed all that. The victory restored pride in the United States. The nation made sure that the Persian Gulf War veterans felt honored when they returned home. The first troops returned March 8, 1991. Many were greeted with cheers and streams of yellow ribbon. The celebrations continued through April and May as more troops returned home.

Operation Desert Storm restored America's pride.

The official Welcome Home celebration occurred June 15, 1991, in Washington, D.C. General Schwarzkopf led more than 8,000 troops down Constitution Avenue to the Pentagon. Nearly 200,000 flag-wavers cheered. M1A1 tanks rumbled by. Stealth fighters flew overhead.

A week later, Schwarzkopf and his men went to New York City. There they received a ticker-tape parade. Americans cheered for more than just a victory. They cheered for their country.

The United States knew the risks involved in the Persian Gulf War. They remembered the lives lost in Vietnam. Yet they were willing to risk it all again. Americans had turned back Iraq's war machine. They had stopped Saddam Hussein from controling Kuwait's oil supply. Operation Desert Storm made it all possible.

*American troops received a much-deserved
ticker-tape parade in New York City.*

Life Goes On

Mike Kenny and Mike Beguelin were Harrier
pilots for the Marine Corps in Operation Desert
Storm. They flew 73 combat missions. Once, enemy
flak nearly hit Beguelin's aircraft. Both pilots returned
home uninjured. But two of their comrades were
killed.

"It makes you realize that you're just a speck of dust
and that there's nothing keeping you around except
some good luck," Beguelin said. He plans to spend
more time with his wife, Cheryl. "I'm gonna buy her a
flower," he said, "take her out to dinner, and let her
know how important she is in my life."

"The war's taught me the sky's the limit," said Kenny.
"I can do anything."

§

Major Dave Johnson is a Marine helicopter pilot. He
had never been in combat before Operation Desert
Storm.

On Day 3 of the ground war, while delivering troops to Kuwait, he came under enemy fire.

"Rounds started landing close enough for us to know that they were being aimed at us," he said. "Mostly it was real interesting. It wasn't scary or alarming. I had known what was going on and how to do what I was supposed to do. I took care of business."

§

Major Jane Fisher is an F-15 maintenance supervisor. She spent seven months in Saudi Arabia, the country south of Kuwait. She left her 11-year-old son, Jayson, and 4-year-old daughter, Mary Jean, in the care of her husband, Henry.

When Fisher returned to Langley Air Force Base in Hampton, Virginia, her family greeted her. "I saw Henry holding Mary," she recalled. "I thought, 'Oh, gosh, I don't want to cry in front of all these people.'"

Fisher is making up for lost time with her family.
"Jayson is not comfortable with me yet," Fisher said.
"He doesn't know whether to put his arms around me or
be tough, be like a man. I don't think Mary will have
any problems."

§

On March 8, 1991, in northern Maine, Jeanette Yates
woke her children at 4 a.m. She wanted them to greet
their father, Captain Rodney Yates, at Langley Air Force
Base. Yates had been away for seven months.

When Captain Yates stepped off the plane, 6-year-old
Esther rushed to her father. She tearfully embraced him.
"She missed him the most, I think," said Jeanette Yates.
"She was real teary-eyed and real emotional."

"There's nothing that could have eclipsed that moment,"
Captain Yates added. "That was a good moment."

§

On February 2, 1991, Marine Captain Jonathan Edwards died when his helicopter gunship crashed in Saudi Arabia. Edwards was from Grand Rapids, Michigan. He was buried in Arlington National Cemetery near Washington, D.C. During the funeral, his 11-year-old son Bennet wept while wearing his father's flight jacket.

Since then, the Edwards family has coped with the loss. Sometimes, it is difficult. "My husband went out in a blaze of glory," said Gayle Edwards. "That's important for the children to have. He was definitely a hero. We try to get over the rough days and share the good ones."

§

Major Sergeant "Butch" Fields is a member of the Air Force fire-fighting outfit. While stationed in the Saudi Arabian Desert, Fields saw a six-week-old white-and-yellow puppy wandering a desert road. The puppy looked lost and confused.

Fields scooped up the puppy and brought him back to camp. Fields, from North Carolina, named the dog "BoJoe." Soon Fields and BoJoe were best friends. "BoJoe was a great tension reliever for everyone," Fields said. "He reminded everyone of a little piece of home."

When Operation Desert Storm ended, Fields got his orders to return home. He wanted to take BoJoe with him. The military could not allow BoJoe on a military airplane.

Fields refused to abandon the dog. He borrowed money from his comrades. He collected the $1,488 needed to ship BoJoe to the United States on a commercial airline.

Fields and BoJoe live at Shaw Air Force Base in Sumter, North Carolina. BoJoe now romps on the grassy fields of the air base. He's far away from the hot Saudi Desert.

IRAQ'S WAR ATROCITIES

Iraq invaded Kuwait to gain more territory. When the Allies forced the Iraqis from Kuwait, the Iraqis made sure the world knew they were not happy to leave.

The most obvious sign of Iraqi spite came in the Burgan oil fields west of Kuwait City. There, the Iraqis set fire to more than 500 oil wells—half of the nation's total. A black-gray oil cloud hung over the fields. The cloud cooled the air temperature by 20 degrees. White-orange fireballs roared from the wells into the sky. Then the fire turned into black columns of acrid smoke. The air was hard to breathe. Everything smelled like oil.

The fires created the greatest oil field disaster. They created the greatest industrial disaster in world history. The extent of environmental damage may never be fully known.

Iraqi soldiers blew up over 500 Kuwaiti oil wells.

The Iraqis also spilled 460 million gallons of oil into the Persian Gulf. The oil slick—the largest ever—spread over 120 miles. It covered beaches and killed wildlife.

Kuwait City held more signs of Iraqi spite. Iraqi soldiers vandalized the city. They damaged all government buildings. They reduced Kuwait's National Museum to rubble. They burned libraries and palaces. They crippled electric, water, and telephone utilities. They stole buses and cabs. Iraqi troops took computers and hospital supplies.

Even worse, Kuwaiti citizens suffered torture, rape, and mass execution. Personal property was stolen. Houses were burned. The Iraqis killed horses and livestock. They took thousands of Kuwaiti citizens as hostages.

Outside Kuwait City stretched the "highway of death." This was a road Allied aircraft bombed and strafed. Charred vehicles jammed the road—vehicles the Iraqi's had stolen as they fled the city.

Some countries criticized the Allies for using such brute force on the fleeing Iraqi's. But then the stories of Iraq's war atrocities became known. Suddenly, many wondered why the Allies hadn't used more force to expel the Iraqis.

THE SECRETS OF
OPRERATION DESERT STORM

Most of what happens during a war isn't known until after the final shots have been fired. That's because war creates much confusion and destruction. Communication breaks down. Other times, information is purposely withheld to protect secret missions. Here are some Operation Desert Storm secrets.

The Gulf War Virus

Weeks before Operation Desert Storm, United States spies placed a computer virus into a computer printer. The printer was sent to Baghdad. The printer was to be used in a military computer network that helped Baghdad's air defenses.

The Iraqis attached the printer to their computer system. The virus worked its way to the main computer. When the Iraqis tried to use the computer system, the virus kept the computer screens blank. According to U.S. officials, the virus did its job.

Taking Aim at Saddam Hussein

After the war ended, President George Bush and his generals denied that the Allies wanted to kill Saddam Hussein. But less than 12 hours before Operation Desert Storm ended, the military sent two special bombs to a U.S. Air Force base deep inside Saudi Arabia.

The laser-guided bombs were called the GBU (Glide Bomb Unit)-28. They were nicknamed the "bunker-busters." They weighed 5,000 pounds and looked like torpedos. The bombs could penetrate hardened Iraqi bunkers—just like the one in which Hussein was reportedly hiding.

Because the bombs were so long and heavy, two F-111 fighter jets were needed. On the night of February 27, the two F-111s took off for the al-Taji Air Base 15 miles northwest of Baghdad. U.S. intelligence officers guessed that Hussein would be at the al-Taji Air Base.

Several hours later, the F-111s released the two GBU-28s. With laser-guided controls, the weapons officers directed the bombs onto their targets.

The bombs crashed through an air duct on the bunker's roof. Seconds later, smoke billowed from the bunker's six entrances.

The bombs destroyed the bunker. But the mission wasn't a complete success. Hussein was not in the bunker.

Iraq's Nuclear Threat

A main military target was Iraq's nuclear weapons factories. Iraq was building its own nuclear program. One day the program would yield atomic weapons.

It was scary to think of Hussein with nuclear weapons. The Allies decided to bomb the factories before he could make any weapons.

The factories were early targets of Desert Storm. The Allies hoped that the bombings would force the Iraqis to give up their nuclear program.

After the war, United Nations (U.N.) inspectors looked over the bombed-out factories. Iraq kept a close watch on the inspectors as they toured the buildings. Officials harrassed the inspectors. They refused to turn over important documents. Once, they detained the inspectors for a weekend. Then they set them free.

Reports by the inspectors showed that the Iraqis still have a nuclear program. They found equipment that makes enriched uranium, a part of nuclear weapons. One document showed Iraqi plans to build a nuclear bomb.

Iraq insists that it has revealed everything about its nuclear program. U.N. inspectors have their doubts. "We need to keep the pressure on," said one inspector. "They haven't given up the program, and that's the scary thing."

COPING IN KUWAIT

The Rebuilding Begins

Before the Iraqi invasion, Kuwait was a wealthy oil kingdom. The royal al-Sabah family ruled Kuwait wisely. Kuwait had modern cities. The citizens received health care, public transportation, jobs, and housing. But the Iraqi invasion changed all that.

The Emir of Kuwait was in exile for seven months while Iraq occupied his country. When he stepped off his plane and onto Kuwaiti soil, he tearfully kissed the runway. The people danced and sang in the streets. Their country had been freed. But it was different. Kuwait was in shambles. There was no water. There was no electricity. There was only smoke from the burning oil fields. It would take $20 billion to rebuild the country.

The Allies helped Kuwait rebuild. American, British, and French companies performed most of the new construction. They delivered electric generators and medical supplies. They repaired oil refineries.

Though the war had reduced Kuwait's oil production, oil shipments resumed less than three months after the Iraqis left Kuwait. To clean up the oil slick along the Kuwaiti coast, British military volunteers scoured the beaches.

The Allies also established food distribution points. But there were long lines. Often, there wasn't enough food for everyone.

Many Kuwaitis scavenged for the goods they needed. They stripped parts from abandoned and burned-out cars. Garbage went uncollected. The bodies of dead Iraqi soldiers were dragged outside towns and cities.

Kuwaitis took out their anger on the many Middle East foreigners who lived in their country. Some were beaten. Those suspected of helping the Iraqis during the war were tortured. Nearly 200,000 Palestinians fled the country, fearing for their lives.

Fighting Fire With Fire

To put out the oil well fires, Kuwait hired eight teams of firefighters from Canada and the United States. They also hired the world famous Red Adair Company. But before any fires could be put out, soldiers had to clear mine fields and booby traps.

Once the mines were cleared, the firefighting teams went in. They had their work cut out for them. The fires reached temperatures of 4,000 degrees Fahrenheit. The fires turned the sand into liquid glass. Even more deadly was the gas that hung in the air. The threat of explosions was constant.

The teams used two firefighting methods. One method poured large amounts of water on a blaze. This lowered the temperature so the oil couldn't ignite. Most well fires were put out this way.

For the stubborn fires, the teams used a more drastic method. The fire fighters fastened high-explosives to the end of a 60-foot pole called a "boom." The boom was attached to a bulldozer.

*U.S. and Canadian firefighters helped
put out the Kuwaiti oil well fires.*

The explosives were placed over the wellhead. Crews sprayed the driver with water to keep him cool. Then the driver set off the explosives. The force of the explosion suffocated the fire—like blowing out a candle. Once the fire was out, four men rushed the well. They installed a new well valve. Then the men closed the valve to stop the flow of oil.

Some fires took days to put out. Others took months. Many said it would take over a year to extinguish all the fires. But by the end of 1991, firefighters had put out all Kuwaiti oil fires.

A New Kuwait?

After the war, the royal family had promised to restore the 1962 Constitution. (The Constitution had been suspended in 1986.) Instead, they imposed martial law. The Kuwaiti's had hoped that changes would be made. They wanted more voting rights. They wanted the royal family to loosen their grip on the economy. They wanted more private ownership of businesses. But now they fear that government rule will remain the same.

*After Desert Storm, many Kuwaitis
wondered about their future.*

IRAQ REGROUPS

When the war ended, the Allies kept some troops in Kuwait. They wanted to make sure Saddam Hussein did not regroup for another attack.

Meanwhile, Iraq struggled to rebuild. The Allies had knocked out electricity, water, and telephone lines. They had destroyed bridges. Fuel was scarce. The Allies also destroyed Iraq's oil refineries. Iraq could not import oil.

Even worse, medicine was scarce. Outbreaks of diseases were common. There was not enough food. And the black market thrived. Some goods cost 50 times the normal price. It will take a long time before Iraq returns to its prewar way of life. Some say it will cost over $100 billion to rebuild Iraq.

Rebellion

On March 3, 1991, Iraq signed a cease-fire agreement with the Allies. A few weeks later, Iraq faced a threat of civil war. The Kurds, a non-Arab tribal people in northern Iraq, started a rebellion. At the same time, the Shiites, a Moslem sect, rebelled in the south.

Neither the Kurds nor the Shiites wanted Hussein to remain in power. The Allies hoped the rebellion would be successful. But the Allies refused to join the rebellion.

Hussein responded harshly to the uprising. He sent helicopter gunships to bomb and strafe the rebels. (The Allies had agreed to let the Iraqis fly their helicopters. The use of airplanes was forbidden.) In Baghdad, Army troops patrolled the streets. They manned roadblocks at the city's entrances.

At first, the rebels captured many towns and villages. But the relentless pounding by the gunships proved to be too much. Even worse, Hussein's Army used some heavy armor that had survived the war. The Shiite rebellion fizzled. But the Shiites' presence in the south remains.

The Kurds, however, put up a greater fight. They controlled the northern mountain region. Iraq's heavy armor found it hard to wage war there. And the Kurds could easily hide. The Kurds still control the north.

They live in tent villages. But they suffer from the elements, and a lack of food, clothing, and medicine.

There is talk among the Allies of sending weapons and supplies to the Kurds. But so far it is only talk. Meanwhile, the Kurds sit and wait. They wonder what is going to happen next.

What Next, Saddam?

A year after Operation Desert Storm ended, not much has changed in Iraq. Hussein is still in power. He still has his Republican Guard. He still has his giant posters on Baghdad's street corners. He has survived plots against his life and a civil war. He has survived over 100,000 missions by Allied bombers.

How long Saddam Hussein remains in power is anyone's guess. He won't go easily. And even if he does go, Iraq will probably find itself in another civil war.

GLOSSARY

ALLIED—Military forces from different countries united
    in a common cause.

ARMORED—Vehicles clad with a tough, protective covering.

ATROCITY—Extremely evil or cruel behavior.

BLACK MARKET—An illegal market in which goods are
    sold in violation of price controls and other restrictions.

CRUISE MISSILES—Low-flying missiles that are guided
    by their own computer.

EMIR—An Arabian prince, chieftain, or governor.

FLAK—Exploding shells and missiles from air defense
    guns and rocket launchers.

FRIENDLY FIRE—When troops are killed by their own
    firepower, officially known as "fratricide."

GROUND WAR—A part of the war that involves tanks,
    artillery, armored vehicles, and foot soldiers.

GUNNER—A soldier who fires the gun(s) on a
military vehicle.

KURDS—A non-Arab tribal people.

MARTIAL LAW—Temporary rule by military
authorities over a civilian population.

MOSLEM—A believer in Islam.

PRISONERS OF WAR (POWs)—Soldiers taken prisoner
by the opposing military.

SHIITES—A Moslem sect.

SMART BOMBS—Bombs that use guidance devices.

STEALTH FIGHTER—A military aircraft that cannot be
detected by radar.

STRAFE—To attack with machine-gun fire from low-
flying aircraft.

TAWAKALNA—A division of Iraq's Republican Guard.